SMALL GROUP SERIES

Parenting

Raising Faithful Children in a Fragmented World

Emily Demuth Ishida

Augsburg Fortress, Minneapolis

Contents

INTERSECTIONS
Small Group Series

Parenting
Raising Faithful Children in a Fragmented World

Developed in cooperation with the Division for Congregational Ministries

George S. Johnson, series introduction
Randi Sundet Griner, Andrea Lee Schieber, James Satter, and Eileen K. Zahn, editors
The Wells Group, series design
Mike Mihelich, cover design
PhotoDisc, Inc., cover photo, pp. 35, 43
Graphics for Worship, copyright © 1996, Augsburg Fortress, baptismal symbol on pp. 3, 17, 21, 27, 37, 40, 49
Brian Jensen, RKB Studios, Inc., illustration on p. 18

The developmental assets described on p. 4 are courtesy of Search Institute, and used by permission.

Materials identified as *LBW* are from *Lutheran Book of Worship*, copyright 1978.

Scripture quotations are from New Revised Standard Version Bible, copyright 1989 Division of Christian Education of the National Council of the Churches of Christ in the United States of America. Used by permission.

Introduction

Godly children are not angelic children any more than we as Christian parents are always saints. But imperfect as we are, we can help nurture our children's spiritual lives.

Our children's lives are fragmented—divided between school, church, sports, clubs, and other activities, as well as being influenced by peers, radio, television, the Internet, and other media. What messages do our children get from all of these areas? What unity do they find in their lives? How can we help provide grounding so that, in whatever facets of life they are involved, our children can live faithfully as children of God? It is only with God's help, and through the grace bestowed in Baptism, that we are able to instill in our children a love for God and an understanding of what it means to be a Christian in the world today.

It is a challenge to teach discernment and to learn a value system that is very different from what is portrayed in many movies, television programs, and video games. But every step forward we make with our children becomes a step forward in our own faith, as we learn to articulate and better understand our own relationship with God. It is critical to remember that we need not, indeed we cannot, raise faithful children alone.

Journal keeping

Throughout this course, journal-keeping will be encouraged. Writing might take place when the group is together or individually between sessions, sometimes with specific direction for assignments. It is important to note that some, but not all, participants will welcome this form of reflection. Do not make it mandatory, but encourage and affirm efforts.

Developmental assets

Search Institute, a research and educational organization in Minneapolis, has compiled a list of 40 developmental assets for children. (See page 4.) These assets are components identified in the lives of healthy, happy, well-adjusted children. They are named in this course as an awareness-raising guide as we work to raise healthy, faithful children.

Baptismal promises

This baptismal symbol appears in each chapter next to activities that remind us of the promises we make when our children are baptized.

Developmental Assets

	ASSET TYPE	ASSET NAME	ASSET DEFINITION
EXTERNAL ASSETS	SUPPORT	1. Family support 2. Positive family communication 3. Other adult relationships 4. Caring neighborhood 5. Caring school climate 6. Parent involvement in schooling	Family life provides high levels of love and support. Parent(s) and child communicate positively. Child is willing to seek parent(s) advice and counsel. Child receives support from nonparent adults. Child experiences caring neighbors. School provides a caring, encouraging environment. Parent(s) are actively involved in helping child succeed in school.
	EMPOWERMENT	7. Community values children 8. Children given useful roles 9. Service to others 10. Safety	Child feels that the community values and appreciates children. Child is included in family decisions and is given useful roles at home and in the community. Child and parent(s) serve others and the community. Child is safe at home, at school, and in the neighborhood.
	BOUNDARIES AND EXPECTATIONS	11. Family boundaries 12. School boundaries 13. Neighborhood boundaries 14. Adult role models 15. Positive peer interactions 16. Expectations for growth	Family has clear rules and consequences, and monitors the child's whereabouts. School provides clear rules and consequences. Neighbors take responsibility for monitoring the child's behavior. Parent(s) and other adults model positive, responsible behavior. Child plays with children who model responsible behavior. Adults have realistic expectations of development at this age. Parent(s), caregivers, and other adults encourage child to achieve and develop his or her unique talents.
	CONSTRUCTIVE USE OF TIME	17. Creative activities 18. Child programs 19. Religious community 20. Positive, supervised time at home	Child participates in music, arts, or drama three or more hours each week through home and out-of-home activities. Child spends one hour or more per week in extracurricular school activities or structured community programs. Family attends religious programs or services for at least one hour per week. Child spends most evenings and weekends at home with parent(s) in predictable and enjoyable routines.
INTERNAL ASSETS	COMMITMENT TO LEARNING	21. Achievement motivation 22. School engagement 23. Homework 24. Bonding to school 25. Reading for pleasure	Child is motivated to do well in school. Child is responsive, attentive, and actively engaged in learning. Child does homework when it is assigned. Child cares about her or his school. Child and a caring adult read together for at least 30 minutes a day. Child also enjoys reading without an adult's involvement.
	POSITIVE VALUES	26. Caring 27. Equality and social justice 28. Integrity 29. Honesty 30. Responsibility 31. Healthy lifestyle and sexual attitudes	Child is encouraged to help other people and to share her or his possessions. Child begins to show interest in making the community a better place. Child begins to act on convictions and stand up for her or his beliefs. Child begins to value honesty and act accordingly. Child begins to accept and take personal responsibility for age-appropriate tasks. Child begins to value good health habits. Child learns healthy sexual attitudes and beliefs and to respect others.
	SOCIAL COMPETENCIES	32. Planning and decision-making 33. Interpersonal competence 34. Cultural competence 35. Resistance skills 36. Peaceful conflict resolution	Child learns beginning skills of how to plan ahead and make decisions at an appropriate developmental level. Child interacts with adults and children and can make friends. Child expresses and articulates feelings in appropriate ways and empathizes with others. Child has knowledge of and comfort with people of different cultural/racial/ethnic backgrounds. Child begins to develop the ability to resist negative peer pressure and dangerous situations. Child attempts to resolve conflict nonviolently.
	POSITIVE IDENTITY	37. Personal power 38. Self-esteem 39. Sense of purpose 40. Positive view of personal future	Child begins to feel he or she has control over "things that happen to me." Child begins to manage life's frustrations and challenges in ways that have positive results for the child and others. Child reports having a high self-esteem. Child reports that "my life has a purpose." Child is optimistic about her or his personal future.

SMALL GROUP SERIES

Welcome into the family of those who are part of small groups! Intersections Small Group Series will help you and other members of your group build relationships and discover ways to connect the Christian faith with your everyday life.

This book is prepared for those who want to make a difference in this world, who want to grow in their Christian faith, as well as for those who are beginning to explore the Christian faith. The information in this introduction to the Intersections small-group experience can help your group make the most out of your time together.

Biblical encouragement

"Do not be conformed to this world, but be transformed by the renewing of your minds, so that you may discern what is the will of God—what is good and acceptable and perfect" Romans 12:2.

Small groups provide an atmosphere where the Holy Spirit can transform lives. As you share your life stories and learn together, God's Spirit can work to enlighten and direct you.

Strength is provided to face the pressures to conform to forces and influences that are opposed to what is "good and acceptable and perfect." To "be transformed" is an ongoing experience of God's grace as we take up the cross and follow Jesus. Changed lives happen as we live in community with one another. Small groups encourage such change and growth.

What is a small group?

A number of definitions and descriptions of the small-group ministry experience exist throughout the church. Roberta Hestenes, a Presbyterian pastor and author, defines a small group as an intentional face-to-face gathering of three to twelve people who meet regularly with the common purpose of discovering and growing in the possibilities of the abundant life.

Whatever definition you use, the following characteristics are important.

Small—Seven to ten people is ideal so that everyone can be heard and no one's voice is lost. More than twelve members makes genuine caring difficult.

Intentional—Commitment to the group is a high priority.

Personal—Sharing experiences and insights is more important than mastering content.

Conversational—Leaders who facilitate conversation, rather than teach, are the key to encouraging participation.

Friendly—Having a warm, accepting, nonjudgmental atmosphere is essential.

Christ-centered—The small-group experience is biblically based, related to the real world, and founded on Christ.

Features of Intersections Small Group Series

A small group model

A number of small-group ministry models exist. Most models include three types of small groups:

- *Discipleship groups*—where people gather to grow in Christian faith and life;

- *Support and recovery group*s—which focus on special interests, concerns, or needs; and

- *Ministry groups*—which have a task-oriented focus.

Intersections Small Group Series currently offers material for all of these groups.

For discipleship groups, this series offers a variety of courses with Bible study at the center. What makes a discipleship group different from traditional group Bible studies? In discipleship groups, members bring their life experience to the exploration of the biblical material.

For support and recovery groups, Intersections Small Group Series offers topical material to assist group members in dealing with issues related to their common experience, hurt, or interest.

Ministry groups can benefit from an environment that includes prayer, biblical reflection, and relationship building, in addition to their task focus.

Four essentials

Prayer, personal sharing, biblical reflection, and a group ministry task are part of each time you gather. These are all important for Christian community to be experienced. Each of the six chapter themes in each book includes:

- Short prayers to open and close your time together.

- Carefully worded questions to make personal sharing safe, nonthreatening, and voluntary.

- A biblical base from which to understand and discover the power and grace of God. God's word is the compass that keeps the group on course.

- A group ministry task to encourage both individuals and the group as a whole to find ways to put faith into action.

Flexibility

Each book contains six chapter themes that may be covered in six sessions or easily extended for groups that meet for a longer period of time. Each chapter theme is organized around two to three main topics with supplemental material to make it easily adaptable to your small group's needs. You need not use all the material. Most themes will work well for 1½- to 2-hour sessions, but a variety of scheduling options is possible.

Bible-based

Each of the six chapter themes in the book includes one or more Bible texts printed in its entirety from the New Revised Standard Version of the Bible. This makes it easy for all group members to read and learn from the same text. Participants will be encouraged through questions, with exercises, and by other group members to address biblical texts in the context of their own lives.

User-friendly

The material is prepared in such a way that it is easy to follow, practical, and does not require a professional to lead it. Designating one to be the facilitator to guide the group is important, but there is no requirement for this person to be theologically trained or an expert in the course topic. Many times options are given so that no one will feel forced into any set way of responding.

Group goals and process

1. Creating a group covenant or contract for your time together will be important. During your first meeting, discuss these important characteristics of all small groups and decide how your group will handle them.

Confidentiality—Agreeing that sensitive issues that are shared remain in the group.

Regular attendance—Agreeing to make meetings a top priority.

Nonjudgmental behavior—Agreeing to confess one's own shortcomings, if appropriate, not those of others, and not giving advice unless asked for it.

Prayer and support—Being sensitive to one another, listening, becoming a caring community.

Accountability—Being responsible to each other and open to change.

Items in your covenant should be agreed upon by all members. Add to the group covenant as you go along. Space to record key aspects is included in the back of this book. See page 53.

2. Everyone is responsible for the success of the group, but do arrange to have one facilitator who can guide the group process each time you meet.

The facilitator is not a teacher or healer. Teaching, learning, and healing happen from the group experience. The facilitator is more of a shepherd who leads the flock to where they can feed and drink and feel safe.

Remember, an important goal is to experience genuine love and community in a Christ-centered atmosphere. To help make this happen, the facilitator encourages active listening and honest sharing. This person allows the material to facilitate opportunities for self-awareness and interaction with others.

Leadership is shared in a healthy group, but the facilitator is the one designated to set the pace, keep the group focused, and enable the members to support and care for each other.

People need to sense trust and freedom as the group develops; therefore, avoid "shoulds" or "musts" in your group.

3. Taking on a group ministry task can help members of your group balance personal growth with service to others.

In your first session, identify ways your group can offer help to others within the congregation or in your surrounding community. Take time at each meeting to do or arrange for that ministry task. Many times it is in the doing that we discover what we believe or how God is working in our lives.

4. Starting or continuing a personal action plan offers a way to address personal needs that you become aware of in your small-group experience.

For example, you might want to spend more time in conversation with a friend or spouse. Your action plan might state, "I plan to visit with Terry two times before our next small-group meeting."

If you decide to pursue a personal action plan, consider sharing it with your small group. Your group can be helpful in at least three ways: by giving support; helping to define the plan in realistic, measurable ways; and offering a source to whom you can be accountable.

5. Prayer is part of small-group fellowship. There is great power in group prayer, but not everyone feels free to offer spontaneous prayer. That's okay.

Learning to pray aloud takes time and practice. If you feel uncomfortable, start with simple and short prayers. And remember to pray for other members between sessions.

Use page 52 in the back of this book to note prayer requests made by group members.

6. Consider using a journal to help reflect on your experiences and insights between meeting times.

Writing about feelings, ideas, and questions can be one way to express yourself; plus it helps you remember what so often gets lost with time.

The "Daily walk" component includes material that can get your journaling started. This, of course, is up to you and need not be done on any regular schedule. Even doing it once a week can be time well spent.

How to use this book

The material provided for each chapter is organized around some key components. If you are the facilitator for your small group, be sure to read this section carefully.

The facilitator's role is to establish a hospitable atmosphere and set a tone that encourages participants to share, reflect, and listen to each other. Some important practical things can help make this happen.

- Whenever possible meet in homes. Be sure to provide clear directions about how to get there.

- Use name tags for several sessions.

- Place the chairs in a circle and close enough for everyone to hear and feel connected.

- Be sure everyone has access to a book; preparation will pay off.

Welcoming

In this study, parents and guardians of children of any age can come together to explore what it means to be a parent today. Welcome and affirm all who come! Sometimes participants will be asked to work together in smaller groups. It may be helpful in such times for participants to group with others who have children of similar ages.

Make necessary arrangements so that the physical and emotional environment for this group is as relaxed and comfortable as possible. Encourage people to come as they are, whether in business suits or gardening clothes. Make arrangements for child-care options to be available. Seek volunteer caregivers or shared child-care opportunities so that financial constraints do not keep people from attending.

Create a cozy atmosphere. Comfortable seating, and space where everyone can converse with one another and be part of the group is vital. Encourage people to bring photos of their children to share with the group.

Focus

Each of the six chapter themes in this book has a brief focus statement. Read it aloud. It will give everyone a sense of the direction for each session and provide some boundaries so that people will not feel lost or frustrated trying to cover everything. The focus also connects the theme to the course topic.

Community building

This opening activity is crucial to a relaxed, friendly atmosphere. It will prepare the ground for gradual group development. Two "Community building" options are provided under each theme. With the facilitator giving his or her response to the questions first, others are free to follow.

One purpose for this section is to allow everyone to participate as he or she responds to nonthreatening questions. The activity serves as a check-in time when participants are invited to share how things are going or what is new.

Make this time light and fun; remember, humor is a welcome gift. Use fifteen to twenty minutes for this activity in your first few sessions and keep the entire group together.

During your first meeting, encourage group members to write down names and phone numbers (when appropriate) of the other members, so people can keep in touch. Use page 51 for this purpose.

Discovery

This component focuses on exploring the theme for your time together, using material that is read and questions and exercises that encourage sharing of personal insights and experiences.

Reading material includes a Bible text with supplemental passages and commentary written by the topic writer. Have volunteers read the Bible texts aloud. Read the commentary aloud only when it seems helpful. The main passage to be used is printed so that everyone operates from a common translation and sees the text.

"A further look" is included in some places to give you additional study material if time permits. Use it to explore related passages and questions. Be sure to have extra Bibles handy.

Questions and exercises related to the theme will invite personal sharing and storytelling. Keep in mind that as you listen to each other's stories, you are inspired to live more fully in the grace and will of God. Such exchanges make Christianity relevant and transformation more likely to happen. Caring relationships are key to clarifying one's beliefs. Sharing personal experiences and insights is what makes the small group spiritually satisfying.

Most people are open to sharing their life stories, especially if they're given permission to do so and they know someone will actively listen. Starting with the facilitator's response usually works best. On some occasions you may want to break the group into units of three or four persons to explore certain questions. When you reconvene, relate your experience to the whole group. If your group includes couples, encourage them to separate for this smaller group activity. Appoint someone to start the discussion.

Wrap-up

Plan your schedule so that there will be enough time for wrapping up. This time can include work on your group ministry task, review of key discoveries during your time together, identifying personal and prayer concerns, closing prayers, and the Lord's Prayer.

The facilitator can help the group identify and plan its ministry task. Introduce the idea and decide on your group ministry task in the first session. Tasks need not be grandiose. Activities might include:

- Ministry in your community, such as adopting a food shelf, clothes closet, or homeless shelter; sponsoring equipment, food, or clothing drives; or sending members to staff the shelter.

- Ministry to members of the congregation, such as writing notes to those who are ill or bereaved.

- Congregational tasks where volunteers are always needed, such as serving refreshments during the fellowship time after worship, stuffing envelopes for a church mailing, or taking responsibility for altar preparations for one month.

Depending upon the task, you can use part of each meeting time to carry out or plan the task.

In the "Wrap-up," allow time for people to share insights and encouragement and to voice special prayer requests. Just to mention someone who needs prayer is a form of prayer. The "Wrap-up" time may include a brief worship experience with candles, prayers, and singing. You might form a circle and hold hands. Silence can be effective. If you use the Lord's Prayer in your group, select the version that is known in your setting. There is space on page 51 to record the version your group uses. Another closing prayer is also printed on page 51. Before you go, ask members to pray for one another during the week. Remember also any special concerns or prayer requests.

Daily walk

Seven Bible readings and a thought, prayer, and verse for the journey related to the material just discussed are provided for those who want to keep the theme before them between sessions. These brief readings may be used for devotional time. Some group members may want to memorize selected passages. The Bible readings also can be used for supplemental study by the group if needed. Prayer for other group members also can be part of this time of personal reflection.

A word of encouragement

No material is ever complete or perfect for every situation or group. Creativity and imagination will be important gifts for the facilitator to bring to each theme. Keep in mind that it is in community that we are challenged to grow in Jesus Christ. Together we become what we could not become alone. It is God's plan that it be so.

For additional resources and ideas see *Starting Small Groups—and Keeping Them Going* (Minneapolis: Augsburg Fortress, 1995).

1 What Is a Faithful Child?

Focus

In Baptism, parents promise to nurture their children in the Christian faith. Raising children with a spiritual base is a constant challenge in a world that would reject or ignore God.

Community building

Journal-keeping will be encouraged in this course. Encourage, but do not require, participants to bring journals, or have writing paper ready.

Introduce yourselves to one another. Share your children's names and their ages. Look over the following list and share a couple of related anecdotes about your children with the group.

- Currently, my greatest parenting challenge is . . .
- I had a spiritual moment with my child when . . .
- I remember my child's baptism because . . .
- My favorite thing about parenting is . . .
- From this group, I hope to learn . . .

Option

Each stage of a child's development offers its own challenges and rewards. What do you like best about your children's ages? What do you least enjoy about your children's ages?

Your child now

Invite participants to record in their journals a significant anecdote about their child or children.

Opening prayer

God, our heavenly parent, help us to teach our children to lead faithful and godly lives, confident of who they are called to be amidst a world that would ignore you. In Jesus' name we pray. Amen.

Defining a faithful child

Read these directions aloud.

Each of us may have our own ideas about what makes a child faithful or godly. Look over the list that follows and check those items that you would call attributes of a faithful child. Circle the three qualities you consider most important. Add more attributes if you wish. What are some of the things that the group agrees are primary attributes of faithful children? Are some of the attributes on this list irrelevant?

Complete individually, then share responses with the group.

A faithful child . . .

____ is polite and respectful.

____ knows some Bible verses.

____ doesn't fight.

____ knows Bible stories.

____ participates in worship regularly.

____ prays before eating.

____ excels in school.

____ sees the world as God's creation.

____ resists negative peer pressure.

____ has empathy, sensitivity, and friendship skills.

____ has high self-esteem.

____ is able to discern right from wrong.

____ helps around the house.

____ doesn't watch much television.

____ doesn't swear.

____ is neat and clean.

____ can relate to God in everyday life.

____ attends Sunday school and church.

____ helps other people.

____ follows the Ten Commandments.

____ relates well to family members.

____ accepts all people.

____ has been baptized.

____ _____

____ _____

A further look

Within this course, the words *faithful, godly,* and *spiritual* may be used interchangeably, although they may have different nuances for different people.

As a group, create a working definition of a faithful child for your group. Remember, this definition may change as the course progresses.

A faithful child is . . .

_____

_____

Group goals and ministry task

Refer to pages 7 and 8 in this book. Read about group goals and group ministry tasks. Form groups of three to discuss group goals and a group ministry task. Talk about the following question and brainstorming topic. Then come back together as a group.

Couples should join two different groups for activities like this.

- What do you hope to accomplish in this small-group course?

- Brainstorm group ministry task ideas that include the children of group members.

- Bring your ideas to the whole group for discussion and decision-making.

Experiencing ways to reach out in Christ's love is a powerful way to learn. A project involving recycling, or cleaning up a park or roadside, creates an opportunity to talk about being good stewards of the earth. Projects aimed at children, such as collecting children's toys and clothing for a local shelter, may also be appropriate. Record your goals and group ministry task in the appendix on page 53.

Discovery

Matthew 3:13-17

Read this passage aloud.

13 Then Jesus came from Galilee to John at the Jordan, to be baptized by him. 14 John would have prevented him, saying, "I need to be baptized by you, and do you come to me?" 15 But Jesus answered him, "Let it be so now; for it is proper for us in this way to fulfill all righteousness." Then he consented. 16 And when Jesus had been baptized, just as he came up from the water, suddenly the heavens were opened to him and he saw the Spirit of God descending like a dove and alighting on him. 17 And a voice from heaven said, "This is my Son, the Beloved, with whom I am well pleased."

Baptismal grace

Read and discuss.

Jesus' baptism is the first thing we hear about him in his adult life. The passages that precede his baptism recall his birth (Matthew 1, Luke 2) and his visit to the temple as a 12-year-old (Luke 2). Then, suddenly he is an adult being baptized by John the Baptist. What is the significance of this event? Look at Matthew 4:1-11.

- What happened to Jesus immediately after he was baptized?
- How did Jesus' baptism help him face the temptation of the devil?
- How was Jesus equipped for ministry through baptism?
- What part did the Holy Spirit play in Jesus' baptism?

Perhaps not all group members have been baptized or had their children baptized. Focus on the positive aspects of Baptism at any age. Baptism marks a starting point, not an end, in a new relationship with God.

Jesus was blessed by God and received power from the Holy Spirit at his baptism, just before he was tempted. The Holy Spirit strengthened him to resist temptation.

Jesus' baptism equipped him to move forward in his faith journey by the presence of the Holy Spirit within him and the blessing of God upon him.

- How does this compare to the baptisms of our children or our own baptisms?
- What role does the Holy Spirit play in our lives and in the lives of our children?

A further look

After volunteers read the Bible verses aloud, discuss the following questions.

Look up and read aloud these sets of verses: Matthew 28:19-20; Mark 16:16; Romans 6:4; Titus 3:4-8a.

- Where in the Bible is there a clear command to baptize in the name of the Father, Son, and Holy Spirit?
- What are some of the benefits of Holy Baptism?
- How will baptism (our own and our children's) help us raise faithful children?

Reviewing our spiritual journey

Have two people read
the following vignettes
to the group.

Amelia grew up in a small, rural community in the late 1960s
and early 1970s. "Everyone went to church—different denomi-
nations, but all Christian. Most of my schoolmates were well-
versed in the Ten Commandments and the Lord's Prayer and
the real meaning of Christmas. Wednesday evenings were
reserved for confirmation class and church events, so none of
the area schools scheduled activities then. The businesses in
town closed from 12:00 to 3:00 on Good Friday, and of course
stores were never open on Sundays.

"Now I look at my own children—the neighborhood kids they
play with are Muslim, Christian, Jewish, or no religion at all;
on the way to church on Sunday mornings we drive past
parks full of kids playing in soccer leagues; Christmas is over-
whelmed by the holiday items that crowd the stores from Sep-
tember on, and in a half-hour of television they can see all ten
of the Commandments violated!"

Joel tells his story: "My folks never were much for church.
I was baptized as a child and went to church with them a
couple times during the year. Mostly, Dad liked to sleep in
on Sundays, and I think my mother didn't have the energy
to get us all cleaned up and off to church. I didn't really know
much about the Christian faith until I went to college.

"I attended a Christian college not far from my home, and religion classes were part of the requirements. The more I learned
about God, the more I wanted to know. I found real joy and
peace in a God who seeks us out and calls us his children.

"Now I have two young children, and I'm wondering how I
can instill in them the joy of living as a child of God. My own
faith is rich, but I haven't learned to talk about it in child's
terms. I don't remember hearing my parents talk about God
with me."

Compare and contrast these two vignettes with your own childhood and adulthood. What are your memories? Form groups of three and share your answers to the following questions with one another. You may have more than one answer for each statement.

■ Compared with my childhood, my child . . .

a. has a clearer understanding of the Christian faith.
b. is exposed to more things that conflict with leading a godly life.
c. has more time reserved for church activities.
d. has less time for church.

■ My parents or caregivers . . .

a. attended church with me regularly.
b. took me to Sunday school and confirmation, but never talked about God themselves.
c. stayed away from any church activities.
d. showed me how to integrate my Christian faith into my whole life.
e. let me choose my own religious beliefs.

■ My children . . .

a. attend church with me regularly.
b. are familiar with Bible stories and the Christian faith.
c. see their parents living out their faith every day.
d. are unfamiliar with the church, worship services, and devotional lives.

■ As a parent, I . . .

a. feel ill-equipped to share God with my children.
b. often talk about my faith or show my faith through my actions.
c. have occasionally discussed God with my children.
d. am confident my children will get all the spiritual instruction they need from church.
e. want to protect my children (from pain, drugs, cults, harmful relationships, and so forth).

Raising a faithful child appears to be a daunting task. But we take a major step of that journey when we bring our children to be baptized. We cannot raise our children alone. We need God's blessing on our children, and we need to be connected to a community of believers. Our children need the Holy Spirit within them to lead a godly life.

Read aloud.

Consider this

As we parent, the developmental assets identified by Search Institute can serve as a helpful guide. Raising godly children means raising children who are well-adjusted in all aspects of their lives. In each of the chapters, a link will be made to groupings of these assets.

Search Institute lists "Support" as a category of external assets that children need for healthy development. See items 1-6 on page 4 of the introduction.

- **How does family support, positive family communication, and a caring neighborhood help in the healthy spiritual development of children?**

- **What might a lack of support in one of these areas mean for the other areas of support?**

Faith journey

Read aloud and discuss.

When parents bring infants and young children to Baptism, they promise to continue to walk a journey of faith together with their children. This journey involves teaching the children the tenets of the faith: the Lord's Prayer, the Apostles' Creed, the Ten Commandments, and the Bible. Baptismal sponsors also promise to walk this path.

Between now and the next group meeting, take time to reflect upon your own faith journey. If you wish, write about it in your journal, or reflect upon your experiences and be ready to talk about whatever you feel comfortable to share. You might describe how your spiritual upbringing differs from that of your own child's so far. Or how does it differ from the vignettes?

Remembering Baptism

Water is found near the entrances of some church sanctuaries. People going into worship dip their hands in the water and make the sign of the cross on their forehead. Sometimes we make the sign of the cross at other times in worship, too. We can remember our baptisms each time we make the sign of the cross.

If any group members have children who are not yet been baptized, affirm prior experiences, invite questions, and encourage further individual explorations. Assist in linking group members who so desire, with a pastor.

Remembering Baptism is important. Baptism does not guarantee a perfect life on earth or a ticket to heaven thereafter. In Baptism, God's grace and the forgiveness of sins is proclaimed. In Baptism, the Holy Spirit prepares us to face the temptations of the world. Remembering our baptisms strengthens our relationship with God.

- How can we remember our baptisms and remind our children (and ourselves!) of what it means to be a child of God?

- What could happen on baptismal anniversaries?

Discuss the tradition of celebrating baptismal anniversaries. Introduce this dessert as one way to do this. If you wish, prepare this dessert to enjoy together during this session.

Consider this

Celebrate your child's baptismal anniversary with "Good Soil Cake." (See recipe on page 18.) Read the parable of the sower found in Luke 8:4-15 or use a version of the story rewritten for children. Strive to encourage and nurture your children to be the "good soil" that hears God's word and keeps it.

Recipe for Good Soil Cake

1 large package of chocolate sandwich cookies

½ stick of butter or margarine

8 oz. (224 g) cream cheese

1 c. (240 ml) powdered sugar

2 packs (small, 4-serving size) instant vanilla pudding

3 cups (720 ml) milk

12 oz. (336 g) whipped topping

8-inch diameter (20 cm) new or very clean plastic flower pot. Place waxed paper or a plastic lid from a container such as margarine, on bottom to cover the drainage holes.

artificial flowers

Crush cookies. Mix together butter, cream cheese, and sugar. Separately, combine milk and pudding mix. Fold in whipped topping. Fold the two mixes together. Alternate layers of crushed cookies and cream mix in the plastic flower pot, ending with cookies. Add artificial flowers. Chill. Serve with spoon or plastic trowel.

Wrap-up

See page 10 in the intro-
duction for a description
of "Wrap-up."

Before you go, take time for the following:

■ **Group ministry task**

■ **Review**

See page 51 for sug-
gested closing prayers.
Page 52 can be used for
listing ongoing prayer
requests.

■ **Personal concerns and prayer concerns**

■ **Closing prayers**

Daily walk

Bible readings

Day 1
Proverbs 22:6

Day 2
Mark 1:9-15

Day 3
Galatians 3:25-29

Day 4
Ephesians 6:1-4

Day 5
Peter 3:8-22

Day 6
John 3:1-3

Day 7
John 5:1-5

Verse for the journey

"Therefore we have been buried with him by baptism into
death, so that, just as Christ was raised from the dead by the
glory of the Father, so we too might walk in newness of life"
(Romans 6:4).

Thought for the journey

"Satan, be warned! If you touch any of the baptized, you are
touching the apple of God's eye. He and we are they for
whom Jesus prayed and is praying still."

Baptismal prayer by Rev. Ray Geist, New Brighton, Minnesota.

Prayer for the journey

"Almighty God, heavenly Father, you have blessed us with the
joy and care of children. As we bring them up, give us calm
strength and patient wisdom, that we may teach them to love
whatever is just and true and good, following the example of
our Savior Jesus Christ."

Lutheran Book of Worship, p. 51.

2 Faith as a Child

While striving to raise our children in the Christian faith, we take opportunities to celebrate the faithfulness they already have and explore together the beliefs of the church.

Community building

Option

Describe the family in which you were raised: parents or guardians, siblings. How is your current family similar? How is it different?

- Think about experiences you have had with your children since the last meeting. Were these experiences spiritual? In what way?

- What experiences from your own childhood are particularly memorable? How were they spiritual?

- Share portions of your faith story with the group. (If you have recorded some of this in a journal, you might read aloud a portion of your writing.)

For each question below, choose the statement that most closely fits your child.

My child . . .

a. believed in Santa Claus easily for many years.
b. believed in Santa skeptically; we had to really convince him/her.
c. was never convinced that Santa existed, despite what we said.
d. never believed in Santa Claus because we chose not to encourage such belief.

What about the tooth fairy or the Easter bunny? Did your child believe . . .

a. wholeheartedly?
b. skeptically?
c. not at all?

Discovery

Do you believe?

Read aloud, then invite people to share examples from personal experiences.

Santa Claus. The Easter bunny. The tooth fairy. The sandman. Our children's lives abound with imaginary folks, whether we perpetuate the myths or they are learned from somewhere else.

Many young children believe such stories easily. They have not yet developed the reasoning skills to calculate that Santa Claus can't possibly stop at every house in the world on Christmas Eve!

By the same token, it is sometimes easier for a child to believe the faith stories that we teach than for we ourselves to believe. Whereas we might try to use reason and logic to sort out the story of Jesus' birth, a child often can simply embrace the story and take it to heart. It is important to remember that children are, by nature, imaginative and creative. Such thinking is critical in their development.

Mark 10:13-16

Have two participants read this passage together, one as narrator and the other as Jesus.

13 People were bringing little children to [Jesus] in order that he might touch them; and the disciples spoke sternly to them. 14 But when Jesus saw this, he was indignant and said to them, "Let the little children come to me; do not stop them; for it is to such as these that the kingdom of God belongs. 15 Truly I tell you, whoever does not receive the kingdom of God as a little child will never enter it." 16 And he took them up in his arms, laid his hands on them, and blessed them.

Jesus blesses the children

Read aloud, then invite responses to the questions.

Reading this passage, one might panic, thinking, "I'd better behave like a child or I will never get into heaven!" What does the Bible passage really mean? What did the children have to

Welcome the questions of your children. Children should never be discouraged from asking questions. Discuss ways you can become comfortable dealing with children's questions that might require an answer of "I don't know."

offer to Jesus? What did the children hope to receive from Jesus? What about the others who came to Jesus seeking to earn the kingdom for themselves?

Receiving the kingdom of God as a child means . . .

    a. to believe in God before you are an adult.
    b. to believe without question.
    c. to receive the kingdom as a gift, without the merit of earning it.
    d. to embrace God with openness and receptivity.
    e. other.

Consider this

When Mark died, his three children (Caleb, 11, Rachel, 6, and Isaac, 2) were left without a father. Mark had had diabetes since the age of 9, and his body had rejected the kidney and pancreas transplant he had received 15 months before his death. As family and friends gathered at the funeral home to grieve the loss of Mark, Caleb handed out a paper with these words he had written: "Remember that what is here is only a shell. Mark is in God's hands now. We'll all see him again someday."

Later that week, Rachel said to her aunt, "I wish there was a phone number in heaven where I could call Daddy."

◼ Discuss the depth of faith expressed by Caleb and Rachel.

◼ How can we encourage our children to grow in their faith in times of sadness?

Faith as a child

Read aloud and discuss together.

In 1960, six-year-old Ruby Bridges became one of the first African American children to attend a predominantly white school in New Orleans. All the white parents pulled their children out of school in protest. For Ruby to attend school, she had to walk through a mob of angry white protesters, who held up hateful signs and shouted racial slurs as young Ruby, guarded by federal marshals, walked into the school building.

How did such a young child have the fortitude to walk through the angry mob day after day? Ruby's family attended church regularly. "We wanted our children to be near God's spirit," Ruby's mother said. "We wanted them to start feeling close to him from the very start."

Ruby's faith strengthened and preserved her in a way that amazed even the psychiatrist who visited her. Her relationship to God was such that each day, on the way to school and on the way home, she prayed for the angry people who shouted at her. She asked God to forgive them.

For more information about Ruby Bridges, read *The Story of Ruby Bridges* by Robert Coles (New York: Scholastic, 1995). See Ruby's complete prayer in the "Daily walk" section of this chapter.

- Tell about a time when you forgave someone who had hurt you. What were the challenges for you? Was God part of the process? How?

- When have your children surprised you regarding their understanding or insight about faith? Have they ever shown more compassion, forgiveness, or understanding than you were able to show? When?

- How did God work through Ruby Bridges? How does God work through our own children—perhaps in less dramatic ways?

A further look

Explore and relate. Form groups of three to discuss the questions, then report to the whole group.

Read the story of Samuel and Eli found in 1 Samuel 3:1-8. In this story God speaks through young Samuel, even to deliver news against Eli, his mentor. The child's pure heart is able to hear and receive God's word. How is this story similar to the story of Ruby Bridges?

Samuel's mother had prayed for a child and promised to dedicate the child to God if she should be blessed with one (1 Samuel 1:11). How could you use this creed to help explain the Christian faith to your child?

- What role did the mothers play in the stories of Samuel and Ruby?

- Tell about parents or grandparents who have had an impact on you or someone you know.

- Another verse to read and ponder is Isaiah 11:6. How do we learn from our children?

What we believe

Have a worship book on hand. Ask a volunteer to read the Apostles' Creed aloud to the group.

Despite the amazing perceptions of our children, and how they can soak up more of the faith than we imagine, we may still have problems talking about our own beliefs with our children.

Stating the facts and faith of Christianity is not easy. Christians wrestled with this problem almost 2000 years ago, and they still wrestle with it today. One solution they developed is the Apostles' Creed.

The Apostles' Creed summarizes the essential elements of our Christian faith—belief in God, the Father—creator of the universe; in Jesus Christ—God's only Son, who was born, suffered, died, was buried, and rose again; and in the Holy Spirit, who continues to inspire the church and all believers.

Discuss.

- Is the Apostles' Creed written in words your daughter or son could understand? Which words would be understood? Which words would need more definition?

- How could you use this creed to help explain the Christian faith to your child?

- What other creeds have you used? What words in such creeds address most effectively what we believe today?

Read aloud and discuss together.

Consider this

Just as our children need self-esteem and personal power, they need to know that the spiritual feelings and beliefs they have are legitimate. Look at the internal assets of positive identity, 37-40, on page 4.

Ruby Bridges certainly showed personal power and a sense of purpose as she walked up the steps to Frantz School. She also showed her spiritual power as she prayed for her persecutors.

- What steps can you take to build your child's confidence and self-esteem, providing encouragement in daily life and in spiritual growth?

Wrap-up

Before you go, take time for the following:

- Group ministry task

- Review

- Personal concerns and prayer concerns

- Closing prayers

Daily walk

Bible readings

Day 1
Isaiah 11:6-9

Day 2
1 Timothy 4:7-8

Day 3
Mark 9:33-37

Day 4
Psalm 8

Day 5
1 John 3:18-24

Day 6
Isaiah 43:10-13

Day 7
Hebrews 11:1-3

Verse for the journey

"You then, my child, be strong in the grace that is in Christ Jesus" (2 Timothy 2:1).

Thought for the journey

"Spiritual development is a natural process which unfolds spontaneously if a child is supported and encouraged. When it is suppressed or inhibited, however, a child is neither adequately equipped to confront religious questions healthily, nor sufficiently secure to get the most out of life."

From *Talking to Your Child about God* by David Heller
(New York: Bantam Books, 1988), p. 5.

Prayer for the journey

"Please, God, try to forgive those people. Because even if they say those bad things, they don't know what they're doing. So you could forgive them, just like you did those folks a long time ago when they said terrible things about you."

—Ruby Bridges, age 6

From *The Story of Ruby Bridges* by Robert Coles
(New York: Scholastic, 1995), p. 23.

3 Great Ways to Live

The framework for living that God outlined in the Ten Commandments and that Jesus upheld in his teaching can guide our children's spiritual journeys and their lives.

Community building

The Ten Commandments can be found in Exodus 20:1-17. They are restated in Deuteronomy 5. Their numbering varies from denomination to denomination. Check with your pastor to learn how they are numbered for use in your worshiping community.

In our first chapter we talked about the importance of Baptism, and in the second chapter we talked about the innate sense of spirituality that children have. Discuss any lingering thoughts and questions from previous sessions. In this chapter we will address the laws that God gave us for living, including the Commandments.

Form groups of two or three and list the Ten Commandments in any order. (Do not look in any books.) Gather together and compare lists.

Look at the descriptions that follow. Choose the answer or answers that best describe your children. Discuss your answers with the group.

My children . . .

Option

Think over the past week. What surprising gifts did your children give you? What did they teach you about yourself? About life? About God?

   a. are familiar with the Ten Commandments.
   b. could list some of the Commandments.
   c. can name and understand all of the Commandments.
   d. have a sense of right and wrong behaviors and actions.
   e. are too young to talk specifically about the Commandments, but they understand behaviors that are "right" and "wrong."

Discuss any lingering thoughts and questions from previous sessions.

Opening prayer

Saving God, you have given the Commandments to show us how to live together. As we strive to obey these commands, help us teach our children also, that they may grow in your way. In Jesus' name we pray. Amen.

Discovery

Exodus 20:1-3

Ask someone to read Exodus 20:1-17. The first three verses are printed here. Note: Have a version of the Ten Commandments that your church uses on hand.

Read and discuss.

¹ Then God spoke with all these words: ² I am the LORD your God, who brought you out of the land of Egypt, out of the house of slavery; ³ you shall have no other gods before me.

God's ways to live well

The Ten Commandments provide ten great ways for people to live in community. Teaching children the Ten Commandments is another baptismal promise.

- Imagine yourself as one of the Israelites receiving the Ten Commandments. In what way might they seem to be an overwhelming burden? How might they be liberating?

- How have you kept or not kept the Ten Commandments during the past week? What about your children?

Read Matthew 5:17-30. In this passage, Jesus reveals the full intent of the Commandments. Not only should we not murder, but we should not be hateful to other people either. Not only is adultery wrong, but even looking at another person with lust is wrong.

- How do these two purposes relate in your own life?

Most of us soon realize that we cannot keep the Commandments. We need Jesus, who is a moral example and an inspiration, as well as the only way in which we can receive forgiveness. But the Commandments continue to have two purposes: To reveal to us our need for Jesus and to show us how to live together in community here on earth.

Teaching our children

Many of us have sung the alphabet song countless times. We have counted and reviewed math facts with our children, and struggled with them as they began to read. But how do we teach the Ten Commandments?

Although our youth may complain about curfews or chores, or having to tell their parents where they are going, these limits do give them a sense of security.

Give participants a few minutes to list rules either verbally in small groups, or individually in journal writing.

What are your "house rules"—the expectations that you have in your household? They can be rules that you grew up with, or rules that you have with your children. Some examples might include: "No TV until your homework is done." "No fighting." "Wash your hands before eating." "Say thank you."

- Talk together about these rules. Are there any that punish or restrict the child? How do the rules help the child?

- Talk about the Ten Commandments as a group. For each Commandment, name household rules you have taught your children that correspond with that Commandment. Use your imagination.

A further look

Discuss.

- How many household rules correspond with one of the Ten Commandments?

A rule about obeying parents, for instance, corresponds with the Commandment to "Honor your father and mother." And "Don't fight" fits with "You shall not murder." (Note: It is possible that a rule relates to more than one Commandment!)

Discovery

Active learning

Read aloud, then form pairs. Encourage parents of children of similar ages to pair up. Content of conversations may vary greatly depending upon the age of the child.

Remember learning math, when three candies plus two candies equaled five (until you ate them)? Many children learn visually or by doing more readily than by hearing. Simply reciting the Ten Commandments with young children is not the best way to teach them, any more than one might teach that $5 + 3 = 8$ by only saying it.

Through our actions and the way that we live, we show our children how to live. How can we take a step toward teaching our children what some of the Commandments are and what they mean?

Form pairs, then discuss or role-play some conversations you might have with your children about the Commandments. An example of such a conversation:

Parent: Please don't hit your brother.

Child: He hit me first!

Parent: We don't hit one another. Jesus teaches us to love one another, and God tells us in the Commandments not to hurt one another. Hurting each other hurts our ability to live together in peaceful community.

Child: But he was being mean to me!

Parent: Well, let's talk about it and see how we can work things out.

A further look

Explore and relate.

The golden rule

Matthew 7:12 states, "In everything do to others as you would have them do to you; for this is the law and the prophets."

This verse is commonly referred to as the "golden rule." Other religions, including Judaism, Hinduism, Buddhism, and Confucianism, have forms of this saying, but most are stated negatively, such as, "Don't do to others what you wouldn't want them to do to you." Jesus presented the golden rule as a positive expectation.

■ How can this verse be a positive teaching tool as we guide our children living as God's children?

The Greatest Commandment

Explore and relate.

When Jesus was asked which of the Commandments was the greatest, he had an easy answer. Read Matthew 22:34-40 to find it.

■ How do all the other Commandments play into these two?

■ How can these Commandments and the golden rule help your children learn to live together in peaceful community? Explain.

■ Do all these rules seem more religious than spiritual or godly? Explain.

■ If we have a rich prayer life and a close relationship with God, but are hateful toward those around us, are we being faithful to God? Explain.

If you wish, record
conversations in
journals.

Before the next session, talk about the Ten Commandments,
the golden rule, or the Greatest Commandment with your children. You might integrate the subject into conversation about
household rules, a news story, or current events in your area.
If you wish, record conversations in journals.

Read aloud and discuss.
Use the space at the
bottom of this page to
record ideas that could
work for your house-
hold.

Consider this

**The internal assets of positive values, 26-31, can be found
on page 4 of the introduction.**

**Caring, integrity, honesty, and responsibility are some of
the positive values that children need.**

- **How do these relate to God's ways for living?**

- **By following God's ways, how might our children
build those positive values?**

Wrap-up

Before you go, take time for the following:

- **Group ministry task**

- **Review**

- **Personal concerns and prayer concerns**

- **Closing prayers**

Daily walk

Bible readings

Day 1
Psalm 119:96-104

Day 2
Deuteronomy 28:9

Day 3
John 15:9-17

Day 4
Ephesians 5:6-14

Day 5
John 14:1-6

Day 6
Philippians 1:27-28

Day 7
1 Peter 2:11-17

Verse for the journey

"You shall love the Lord your God with all your heart, and with all your soul, and with all your mind" (Matthew 22:37).

Thought for the journey

The Ten Commandments and the golden rule are much more about what we should do than what we should not do. Just as we teach our children by encouraging good behavior, rather than simply punishing bad behavior, so does God guide us.

Prayer for the journey

"Oh, my good God and Lord, help us children for we are small and don't yet know the right way that takes us to the Lord. But we want to learn and be obedient and study with the adults the Lord's word. I thank you for everything that you gave us and help us to follow your way. Amen."
—Claudia Haberkamp, age 9, Estrela, Brazil
(translated from Portuguese)

From *Children in Conversations with God* by Anza A. Lema (Geneva, Lutheran World Federation, 1979), p. 51.

4 Media, Materialism, and Mores

The mass media can feed our materialistic instincts and form social mores contrary to those taught by God. Discernment and moderation are needed so that our children can pray "*your* kingdom come."

Community building

Have you had an opportunity to talk about the Ten Commandments or the golden rule with your children since the last session? If so, share the experience with the group.

We've defined faithful children, contemplated a child's spirituality, and discussed God's ways for living. In this chapter, we will address complexities of the fragmented world in which we live.

Name that show

Give the teams five to ten minutes to make their lists.

Form two teams. Each team will need two sheets of paper. On one sheet, list current television shows. On the other sheet, list any shows you can remember that no longer are on network television.

Come together and read off the lists of current television shows.

Option

Name benefits from television that your family has experienced. What negative effects have you experienced? Is there anyone who has decided not to own a television set?

■ Are the lists similar? Which is longer?

■ Which shows listed have you watched? Are the lists primarily adult shows or children's shows?

■ Are the lists of old television shows longer or shorter than the lists of current shows?

■ On the lists, circle those shows that you would allow a child under age ten to watch on a regular basis. Put a star by those shows you would let an older child watch on a regular basis.

- How many shows did you find for the under-ten crowd? The over-ten crowd?

- What are some of the differences in content between past and current show?

Opening prayer

God of wisdom, help us use our gifts of technology and media in ways that glorify you, teaching our children to do the same. In Jesus' name we pray. Amen.

Discovery

Extended family

Take a few minutes to fill out the survey individually, then form groups of three to compare notes and discuss the questions.

Take this electronic media survey. Check those items that you have in your household.

___ television

___ VCR

___ cable or pay-per-view television

___ stereo system

___ radio

___ video game set

___ computer

___ Internet access

Form groups of three and discuss the following questions.

- In which rooms in your home do you have electronic media of any kind?

- How many total hours a week do members of your household spend using these media outlets?

- How, if at all, is your children's media time supervised or limited?

- What role can parents play in helping a young child learn to discern between acceptable or unacceptable program content?

Isaiah 2:3b-4

Read aloud and discuss.

3 . . . For out of Zion shall go forth instruction, and the word of the LORD from Jerusalem. 4 He shall judge between the nations, and shall arbitrate for many peoples; they shall beat their swords into plowshares, and their spears into pruning hooks; nation shall not lift up sword against nation, neither shall they learn war any more.

Neither shall they learn war anymore

In November 1985, U.S. President Ronald Reagan and Soviet Premier Mikhail Gorbachev held their first summit in Geneva, Switzerland. Aimed at arms reduction, their summits marked the beginning of the end of the Cold War.

Rev. Jesse Jackson, who was in Geneva for the occasion, spoke at the Ecumenical Center, which houses the World Council of Churches, the Lutheran World Federation, the World Alliance of Reformed Churches, and other organizations.

Jackson based his speech on Isaiah 2:4. "If a person studies medicine, they'll practice it when they see a bleeding person," Jackson said. "Study elementary education, and you'll try to teach people the basics whether you have a classroom or not. Study war, and eventually you will fight. But Isaiah says no— study war no more!" Jackson thundered.

The superpowers of the 1980s heeded this lesson. How much war and violence are our children "studying" or absorbing from television each week? The National Coalition on Television Violence calculates that the average child will witness more than 200,000 acts of violence on television by age 18. "All television is educational. The question is, 'What does it teach?'" said Nicholas Johnson, former head of the Federal Communications Commission. (From *Selling Out America's Children* by David Walsh (Minneapolis: Fairview Press, 1995, p. 45.)

In addition to physical violence, such as shooting, killing, hitting, and exploding, there is structural violence. Structural violence is a term often used to define anything that keeps people from reaching their full potential. Racism, for instance, which can keep people from one race from full inclusion in the world around them, is structural violence.

From the lists generated earlier, choose a show that most people in the group have seen, then discuss the following questions:

- What kind of violence is portrayed?
- How are perpetrators of violence punished?
- How do characters (men and women, children and parents) show respect for each other?

You may also wish to explore and describe content of video games your children play. Discuss how this and other aspects of our culture (local and world news) elevates violence in our culture.

- How are people of differing ethnic groupings portrayed? Is anything stereotypical or offensive?

- What kinds of sexual ethics are portrayed? What values are being communicated?

- Are the socioeconomic lifestyles shown typical of the diversity present in real life?

- How can we learn the ways of God by watching the show?

Consider this

PhotoDisc, Inc. © 1995

Martin Luther's teachings and the Reformation took hold in the 1500s partly because the printing press was available to spread his ideas. Without the invention of the printing press, he may very well have been burned at the stake, the common punishment for heresy at that time.

- How can computers and the mass media work to an advantage for us and for our children?

Discovery

Mark 10:17-27

After reading the text aloud, discuss the questions that follow.

17 As he was setting out on a journey, a man ran up and knelt before him, and asked him, "Good Teacher, what must I do to inherit eternal life?" 18 Jesus said to him, "Why do you call me good? No one is good but God

alone. [19] You know the commandments: 'You shall not murder; You shall not commit adultery; You shall not steal; You shall not bear false witness; You shall not defraud; Honor your father and your mother.'" [20] He said to him, "Teacher, I have kept all these since my youth." [21] Jesus, looking at him, loved him and said, "You lack one thing; go, sell what you own, and give the money to the poor, and you will have treasure in heaven; then come, follow me." [22] When he heard this, he was shocked and went away grieving, for he had many possessions.

[23] Then Jesus looked around and said to his disciples, "How hard it will be for those who have wealth to enter the kingdom of God!" [24] And the disciples were perplexed at these words. But Jesus said to them again, "Children, how hard it is to enter the kingdom of God! [25] It is easier for a camel to go through the eye of a needle than for someone who is rich to enter the kingdom of God." [26] They were greatly astounded and said to one another, "Then who can be saved?" [27] Jesus looked at them and said, "For mortals it is impossible, but not for God; for God all things are possible."

How do you interpret this passage?

Circle answers that apply, then discuss.

a. We must give away all our possessions.
b. We should use moderation in acquiring things, and we should share our wealth.
c. We must not let our money and possessions mean more to us than God does.
d. We cannot truly follow Jesus by giving up so much, so we should just let God save us.
e. Other.

A further look

Explore and relate.

In Jesus' time, religious teachers taught that wealth was a sign of God's approval. To the disciples surprise, Jesus taught the opposite—that wealth can be a barrier to the kingdom.

■ How does the media influence our purchasing decisions?

■ How do people determine how much "stuff" is enough?

■ How do our children differentiate between wants and needs?

■ What are some healthy limits that can be set regarding material possessions?

■ How can we help our children be good stewards of all they have been given?

The Lord's Prayer

Read aloud and discuss this baptismal promise connection.

On every continent, in countless languages, people pray the Lord's Prayer. Taught by Jesus himself, the Lord's Prayer has been embraced for almost 2000 years. As we baptize our children, we commit ourselves to teaching them this prayer, passing it on to yet another generation.

■ What are some ways to teach children this prayer?

"Give us this day our daily bread" and "Your kingdom come," two parts of the Lord's Prayer, can be related to electronic media.

■ Form a group to discuss each phrase. Come together to share with the whole group.

Read and discuss.

Consider this

Our children need creative and extracurricular activities, a religious community, and supervised time at home. These are some of the external assets listed under "constructive use of time," 17-20, listed on page 4 of the introduction.

These assets offer alternatives to spending time watching television or videos. These outlets allow a child to grow as an individual, to learn to interact with others in non-classroom settings, to build a spiritual base.

The internal assets of social competencies, 32-36, lift up decision-making and resistance skills. Additionally, peaceful conflict resolution is contrary to many of the immediate and violent solutions portrayed on television.

Watch some television shows with your children this week, noting how many incidents of violence, disrespect, or values contrary to those of God's kingdom are displayed.

■ Map out a plan of action to make family viewing productive, rather than destructive.

■ Brainstorm with your children to create a list of alternatives to using electronic media: board games, reading aloud, family walks, crafts, and so forth.

Wrap-up

Before you go, take time for the following:

- Group ministry task

- Review

- Personal concerns and prayer concerns

- Closing prayers

Daily walk

Bible readings

Day 1
1 Timothy 6:6-10

Day 2
1 John 5:1-5

Day 3
James 2:1-9

Day 4
Luke 16:19-31

Day 5
Ecclesiastes 5:10

Day 6
Matthew 6:9-13

Day 7
Acts 4:32-35

Verse for the journey

"And [Jesus] said to them, 'Take care! Be on your guard against all kinds of greed; for one's life does not consist in the abundance of possessions'" (Luke 12:15).

Thought for the journey

"Traditionally, family, church, and school have been the primary influences on a child's intellectual, emotional, and moral development. That is no longer the case. In terms of time spent, the biggest influence is now the television set."

From *Selling Out America's Children* by David Walsh (Minneapolis: Fairview Press, 1995), p. 49.

Prayer for the journey

God of simplicity, be with us as we take the turns of life.
Help us as we seek to find that "just right" place. Amen.

'Tis a gift to be simple, 'Tis a gift to be free;
'Tis a gift to come down where we ought to be.
And when we find ourselves in the place just right,
'Twill be in the valley of love and delight.

The Shaker song "Simple Gifts," from *Peace on Earth* (New York: Doubleday Book for Young Readers, 1992), p. 68.

5 Tough Questions

Guiding our children through tough theological questions, and using the Bible as a helpful tool, is important for our children's spiritual development.

Community building

List the tough questions children have asked on a chalkboard or on newsprint.

Share media comments—results of critical television viewing or changes you are trying to make in your media-using habits.

List some of the tough spiritual or religious questions you or others have encountered: "Where did Grandma go when she died?" "Were there dinosaurs on Noah's ark?" "Why does God let wars happen?" "Why is there hunger in the world?" . . . and so forth. Then try to answer some of the questions as a group. How difficult is it? How might answers vary, depending on who asked the questions and when?

Option

Children often say to themselves or to their parents, "When I'm a parent, I'll never do that!" Tell about a time when you found yourself behaving toward your children in a way that you vowed you would never do when you were a child. What was your reaction?

- _____
  _____
- _____
  _____
- _____
  _____

Opening prayer

All-knowing God, we have so many questions! Guide us as we struggle. Help us to better understand your ways. In Jesus' name we pray. Amen.

Genesis 1:1-5

1 In the beginning when God created the heavens and the earth, 2 the earth was a formless void and darkness covered the face of the deep, while a wind from God swept over the face of the waters. 3 Then God said, "Let there be light"; and there was light. 4 And God saw that the light was good; and God separated the light from the darkness. 5 God called the light Day, and the darkness he called Night. And there was evening and there was morning, the first day.

In the beginning

After reading the Genesis text, discuss these questions as a group.

Continue reading from a Bible the rest of the creation story from Genesis 1:6-31. Just as we started with Jesus' baptism to talk about our children's baptisms as the beginning of their faith journey, so does Genesis become a beginning point to talk about tough faith questions. For certainly, since the beginning of time, Christians have struggled with questions to which they could not find adequate answers.

■ Notice how many times the word *God* appears in this passage. Why do you suppose this is the case? Bearing this in mind, what can we conclude is a primary message of this passage?

■ When did you first hear the story of the creation of the earth and humans found in Genesis 1 and 2? How (if at all) have your feelings or beliefs about it changed since you first heard it? How do your children understand the creation story?

Hearing the creation story as a child, and reading it as a teenager who has studied evolution in school, can elicit very different understandings. But one fact remains unchanged: the word *God* appears 39 times, reminding us that the "who" of creation is much more important than the "how." Many of the questions our children ask will bog us down if we get into the whys and wherefores. Our responses must be honest, even if honesty is to say, "I don't know." But the reassuring truths of God can always come through.

"Why did God make skunks?" a child asks. But a couple of days later you learn that skunks eat grubs. That explained the dug-up yard, and also why God made skunks!

Note that the child didn't ask, "Why are there skunks?" He asked, "Why did God make skunks?" And thus he showed that he already got the message of Genesis 1. God created, God said, God made.

Remember, children and youth will not reflect adult perspectives. Encourage them in their questioning and be careful not to shut them out.

- "Why did God let Grandma die?" "I don't know, but I'm sure she is happy to be with God."

- "Why are there wars?" "I don't know, but I believe they make God unhappy."

How can we encourage our children to explore the Bible as a guide to understanding? The Bible is cherished literature, God's word, with the history and poetry of God's people, the teachings of Jesus, and the writings of Paul, all of which can help us and our children come closer to understanding God. We promise at our children's baptisms to place in their hands the Holy Scriptures.

- Share some of your favorite Bible verses, that could also be shared with your children.

Read aloud and discuss.

Consider this

As spiritual nurturers, we need to worry less about providing the "right" answers than about helping our child ask the right questions. Each question asked by a child is a sign of spiritual growth. Rather than trying to resolve each one, encourage struggles with questions and affirm new discoveries. Sometimes, it is best to say nothing at all. At times, especially as our children approach adolescence, we may realize that answers are more likely to come in conversation with others, such as peers, a thoughtful teacher, or an approachable member of the clergy, for example.

- **How do questions asked by our children reflect spiritual growth?**

- **Tell about some questions your children have asked.**

A further look

Explore and relate.

Jean Grasso Fitzpatrick, author of *Something More, Nurturing Your Child's Spiritual Growth* (New York: Penguin Books, 1991), relates this experience of talking to her children about God:

> I have always tried to convey a sense of God's presence in people and in nature, rather than on some distant heavenly throne. One summer's day, after I had picked up my son from day camp, we were

having lunch at the kitchen table when he burst out indignantly, "The boys at camp say God is invisible!"

"Well, he is—" I began, then stopped myself. "You don't think he is?"

"Of course not," he replied, almost scornfully. "Anyone can see God—the sun, the leaves, the people we love. You know!" (pp. 124-125).

- In what way did the boy show a depth of faith understanding?

- How do children easily see the connection between God and nature?

- In what way can you use nature—God's created world—as a bridge to talking about God with your child?

Discovery

Jesus' teaching methods

Read the whole story first, then read these verses together and discuss them as a group.

Jesus asked questions on 289 instances in the four Gospels. Although some are repeated, more than 200 different questions are asked. Many people like to think of Jesus and the Bible as giving all the answers, so it is sometimes surprising to stop and consider this phenomena.

Jesus asked questions like "What do you think?" (Matthew 21:28), "Who are my mother and my brothers?" (Mark 3:33), and "Is it lawful to cure people on the sabbath or not?" (Luke 14:3). Eventually Jesus tells a parable or speaks other words of wisdom, but he first asks questions.

Luke 24:13-35 tells the story of what happens on the road to Emmaus on Easter evening. Read this story independently or as a group.

Now read verses Luke 24:13-27 aloud, with one person being the narrator, one Jesus, and another Cleopas.

- Who preaches the gospel to whom?

Compare this story to the experience Jean Grasso Fitzpatrick had with her son. In both instances, the gospel, the faith, the godliness came from the "student," not the "teacher."

Oftentimes, teaching spirituality comes not in telling children one thing or another, but in asking them the right questions and letting them express their faith.

- Tell about incidents you have had with your children, when by turning their statements or questions back to them they provided the answers.

Tips for handling tough questions

Discuss these tips as a group. Add more of your own ideas to this list.

■ Listen to the question and affirm its validity.

■ Don't be afraid to say, "I don't know."

■ Explore possible answers together. Consult a reference book or Web site. Ask another person, such as teacher, pastor, or other church staff person.

■ Work to discern the real question. (When a child asks about death, their real concern may be whether Mom or Dad is going to die.)

■ Provide answers relevant to a child's age. (Remember that younger children may have trouble thinking abstractly.)

■ Be inviting and receptive to further questions.

■ Pray for God's guidance!

Consider this

PhotoDisc, Inc. © 1995

Read aloud and discuss.

Read the section "Internal Assets, Commitment to Learning," 21-25, found on page 4 of the introduction. Children need to be actively engaged in school and study, as well as growing in their spiritual lives by asking questions and learning how to think for themselves.

■ **What can we do to encourage and nurture these assets?**

Wrap-up

Before you go, take time for the following:

- Group ministry task

- Review

- Personal concerns and prayer concerns

- Closing prayers

Daily walk

Bible readings

Day 1
Matthew 13:10-17,
34-35

Day 2
James 1:2-8

Day 3
John 1:1-14

Day 4
Matthew 7:7-11

Day 5
Isaiah 40:28

Day 6
Luke 20:1-8

Day 7
Romans 8:38-39

Verse for the journey

"Ask, and it will be given you; search, and you will find; knock, and the door will be opened for you" (Matthew 7:7).

Thought for the Journey

"It is when we are empty-handed that we have the most to offer. As always on the spiritual journey, realizing we do not have all the answers—or that a quick response is inadequate—is not a cause for alarm."

From *Something More* by Jean Grasso Fitzpatrick
(New York: Penguin Books, 1991), p. 186.

Prayer for the journey

May all I say and all I think
be in harmony with thee,
God within me,
God beyond me,
maker of the trees.

—prayer of the Chinook people

From *Peace on Earth* by Bijou Le Tord (New York:
Doubleday Books for Young Readers, 1992), p. 18.

6 Pulling It Together

Focus

As parents, we accompany our children on their faith journeys. What are some guidelines and tools we can use to travel that journey with our children?

Community building

Spirituality of art

Check off items on this list, then discuss the questions at the end.

Option

Sing together one verse of a favorite hymn, such as "Amazing Grace." Have a group member play the hymn on a musical instrument. Now, try singing it with the musical accompaniment. Which is more pleasing?

The words and music of hymns work together to express sacred thoughts. How might accompanying your children on their faith journeys be similar to someone accompanying a song?

What art forms most impress you?

___ symphony orchestras

___ art exhibits

___ jazz bands

___ opera

___ traditional crafts

___ poetry

___ sculpture, carvings

___ textiles, stitchery, embroidery

___ photography

___ fashion

___ gourmet cooking, baking

___ hymns, community singing

___ dance

___ movies

___ literature

___ woodworking

___ other: _____

- How do these art forms, either by doing them or observing them, uplift you? Which of these is more significant, from a child's perspective?

- How can the beauty, precision, intricacy, or other attributes of art help us better understand God, our Creator?

- How can we use these art forms to spiritually nurture our children?

Discovery

Deuteronomy 6:4-9

4 Hear, O Israel: The LORD is our God, the LORD alone. 5 You shall love the LORD your God with all your heart, and with all your soul, and with all your might. 6 Keep these words that I am commanding you today in your heart. 7 Recite them to your children and talk about them when you are at home and when you are away, when you lie down and when you rise. 8 Bind them as a sign on your hand, fix them as an emblem on your forehead, 9 and write them on the doorposts of your house and on your gates.

Discuss ways to visibly put God's word before us and before our children. Reflect on this if you wish, and record ideas in journals.

This passage from Deuteronomy is known as the Shema, which is and has been recited by Orthodox Jews, morning and evening, for hundreds of years. In addition to keeping this law ourselves, we are instructed to teach it to our children. There are many ways that people throughout the ages have done this. In a farmhouse, the words "Anyone unwilling to work should not eat" from 2 Thessalonians 3:10 were pasted in large letters on the kitchen wall. Many Orthodox Jews keep a scroll with the Shema on the doorframes of their homes.

- What is there to gain from putting God's word before us in such a visible way?

Romans 12:9-18

Read aloud and discuss what this means in your household.

9 Let love be genuine; hate what is evil, hold fast to what is good; 10 love one another with mutual affection; outdo one another in showing honor. 11 Do not lag in zeal, be ardent in spirit, serve the Lord. 12 Rejoice in hope, be patient in suffering, persevere in prayer. 13 Contribute to the need of the saints; extend hospitality to strangers.

14 Bless those who persecute you; bless and do not curse them. 15 Rejoice with those who rejoice, weep with those who weep. 16 Live in harmony with one another; do not be haughty, but associate with the lowly; do not claim to be wiser than you are. 17 Do not repay anyone evil for evil, but take thought for what is noble in the sight of all. 18 If it is possible, so far as it depends on you, live peaceably with all.

Be transformed

"But Mom, all my friends watch that show."

"But Dad, everybody does it."

At some point we probably have all heard statements similar to these. Children are anxious to conform, to be like the others, to be part of a group. Paul, in his letter to the Romans, tells us not to be conformed to this age and world but to be transformed. The transformed life is outlined in Romans 12:9-18. We cannot be faithful in a vacuum, but rather show our faith in how we relate to others.

- ■ Look over the verses again and choose a phrase that you find particularly relevant to your family. Share your phrase and reasoning with the group.

Because being a Christian is relational, relating to God and relating to others, involving our children in a community of faith is important. Regularly bringing our children to worship, Sunday school, and confirmation classes, and so forth, helps provide for their instruction in the Christian faith.

What would Jesus do?

Read aloud and discuss.

Have you ever seen the letters WWJD on a bracelet, T-shirt, or other item? WWJD stands for "What would Jesus do?" Although many people know it as a contemporary catchphrase, it originated more than a century ago.

In 1896, Charles M. Sheldon began preaching an unusual series of sermons for his Sunday night services. He wrote a continued story about what happened to a group of people who asked the question "What would Jesus do?" before making decisions in their daily lives. The individuals' actions started a spiritual revolution of sorts, as businessmen found they needed to change their business practices, and rich young women ventured into the slums of the town.

During this discussion, do not lose sight of the question "What DID Jesus do?" Through our baptism into the death and resurrection of Jesus, the Christ, we are gifted with salvation.

The sermons, later published as the book *In His Steps,* became a Christian classic. In the 1950s, the book *What Would Jesus Do?* was written with the same premise. In the 1990s, the letters WWJD began to cycle around again, first among youth groups and then spreading from there.

■ By asking what Jesus would do before acting, how might your life reflect the instructions laid out in Romans 12:9-18?

Consider this

Read aloud and discuss.

Look up the external assets of empowerment, 7–10, and "Boundaries and Expectations," 11–16, found in the introduction on page 4.

As we set boundaries and expectations, we need to work to empower your children in their faith—to give them permission to raise questions and continue to grow on their spiritual journeys.

■ **What can you do to encourage and nurture these assets with your children?**

A further look

Discuss these commandments. How might each one be incorporated into the process of parenting?

Ten commandments for raising a spiritual child

1. Share your faith. Tell your child how God is made real to you and how God helps you each day.

2. Get involved in your church as a family. Reinforce those beliefs you teach at home. Church membership provides security and accountability.

3. Read the Bible in your home. Relate scriptures to life situations and challenge your child to lean on God's word.

4. Teach your child to look for God's love in all situations. Talk frequently about the reality of God's love.

5. Teach your child the importance of an active prayer life. Pray daily as a family and talk openly about answered prayers.

6. Go beyond teaching values by showing your child the ways of love as demonstrated by Jesus and in the New Testament.

7. Root your child in the Christian faith and stand strong as you put your hope in God.

8. Encourage your child when doubts about God's love arise. Questioning can strengthen faith.

9. Talk openly about death as a reality of life and let your child know that eternal life is the hope of our faith.

10. Show your child how to "put feet to faith" as you find ways to serve others.

From Debra Fulghum Bruce and Robert Bruce,
Jacksonville, Florida.

Wrap-up

Before you go, take time for the following:

- Group ministry task

- Review

- Personal concerns and prayer concerns

- Closing prayers

Daily walk

Bible readings

Day 1
Ephesians 4:17—5:2

Day 2
Proverbs 1:7-9

Day 3
Titus 2:11-13

Day 4
1 Peter 5:1-4

Day 5
Psalm 51:10-12

Day 6
Psalm 128

Day 7
1 Thessalonians 5:16-28

Verse for the journey

"Grandchildren are the crown of the aged, and the glory of children is their parents" (Proverbs 17:6).

Thought for the journey

"Children who are securely grounded have the confidence to venture forth because they know the way home. From what is close and dear, parents and children can learn much about God who is infinite and powerful. Using home as the starting point and the end of our theology should not seem so odd."

From *Something More* by Jean Grasso Fitzpatrick (New York: Penguin Books, 1991), p. 186.

Prayer for the journey

Caring God, guide us daily as we strive to raise our children as your faithful children. Grant us patience when we are angry, joy when we are discouraged, wisdom when we are afraid, and grace that we may glorify you. Amen.

Appendix

Group directory

Record information about group members here.

Names	Addresses	Phone numbers

Prayers

■ Closing Prayer

Lord God, you have called your servants to ventures of which we cannot see the ending, by paths as yet untrodden, through perils unknown. Give us faith to go out with good courage, not knowing where we go, but only that your hand is leading us and your love supporting us; through Jesus Christ our Lord. Amen.

From *Lutheran Book of Worship* (page 153) copyright © 1978.

(If you plan to pray the Lord's Prayer, record the version your group uses in the next column.)

■ The Lord's Prayer

Prayer requests

Group commitments

Do not be conformed to this world, but be transformed by the renewing of your minds, so that you may discern what is the will of God—what is good and acceptable and perfect. Romans 12:2.

■ For our time together, we have made the following commitments to each other

■ Goals for our study of this topic are

■ Our group ministry task is

■ My personal action plan is

Coffey, Kathy. *Experiencing God with Your Children*. New York: The Crossroad Publishing Company, 1997.

Coles, Robert. *The Spiritual Life of Children*. Boston: Houghton Mifflin Company, 1990.

_____. *The Story of Ruby Bridges*. New York: Scholastic, Inc., 1995.

Dawn, Marva. *Is It a Lost Cause? Having a Heart for the Church's Children*. Grand Rapids, Mich.: Eerdmans, 1997.

Erickson, Kenneth A. *Helping Children Feel Good about Themselves: A Guide to Building Self-Esteem in the Christian Family*. Minneapolis: Augsburg Fortress, Publishers, 1994.

Erlander, Dan. *Let the Children Come: A Baptism Manual for Parents and Sponsors*. Minneapolis: Augsburg Fortress, Publishers, 1997.

Fitzpatrick, Jean Grasso. *Something More: Nurturing Your Child's Spiritual Growth*. New York: Penguin Books, 1991.

Heller, David. *Talking to Your Children about God*. New York: Bantam Books, 1988.

Lauer, Robert H. and Jeannette C. Lauer. *Becoming Family: How to Build a Stepfamily that Really Works*. Minneapolis: Augsburg Fortress, Publishers, 1999.

Le Tord, Bijou, comp. *Peace on Earth*. New York: Delacorte Press, 1992.

Nelson, Gertrude Mueller. *To Dance with God: Family Ritual and Community Celebration*. New York: Paulist, 1986.

Obsatz, Michael. *Raising Nonviolent Children in a Violent World: A Family Handbook*. Minneapolis: Augsburg Fortress, Publishers, 1998.

Prather, Hugh and Gayle. *Spiritual Parenting*. New York: Crown Publishers, 1996.

Ramshaw, Elaine. *The Godparent Book*. Chicago: LTR, 1993.

Schultze, Quentin J. *Winning Your Kids Back from the Media*. Downers Grove, Ill.: Intervarsity Press, 1994.

Sheldon, Charles M. *In His Steps*. Grand Rapids, Mich.: Baker Book House Company, 1984.

Walsh, David. *Selling Out America's Children*. Minneapolis: Fairview Press, 1995.

Augsburg Fortress Devotionals

Devo'Zine: Just for Teens. Call 888-271-7276. Ask for the Augsburg Fortress edition.

The Home Altar: Devotions for Families with Children. Call 1-800-426-0115, ext. 639.

✂

Please tell us about your experience with INTERSECTIONS.

4. What I like best about my INTERSECTIONS experience is

5. Three things I want to see the same in future INTERSECTIONS books are

6. Three things I might change in future INTERSECTIONS books are

7. Topics I would like developed for new INTERSECTIONS books are

8. Our group had _____ sessions for the six chapters of this book.

9. Other comments I have about INTERSECTIONS are

Thank you for taking the time to fill out and return this questionnaire.

------------------------- FOLD CARD IN HERE, SEAL WITH TAPE, AND MAIL TODAY! -------------------------

Name _____

Address _____

Daytime telephone _____

Please check the INTERSECTIONS book you are evaluating.

☐ The Bible and Life ☐ Following Jesus ☐ Peace
☐ Captive and Free ☐ Integrity ☐ Praying
☐ Caring and Community ☐ Jesus: Divine and Human ☐ Reconcilable Differences
☐ Death and Grief ☐ Managing Stress ☐ Self-Esteem
☐ Divorce ☐ Men and Women ☐ Smart Choices
☐ Faith ☐ Parenting

Please tell us about your small group.

1. Our group had an average attendance of _____ .

2. Our group was made up of
_____ Young adults (19-25 years).
_____ Adults (most between 25-45 years).
_____ Adults (most between 45-60 years).
_____ Adults (most between 60-75 years).
_____ Adults (most 75 and over).
_____ Adults (wide mix of ages).
_____ Men (number) and _____ women (number).

3. Our group (answer as many as apply)
_____ came together for the sole purpose of studying this INTERSECTIONS book.
_____ has decided to study another INTERSECTIONS book.
_____ is an ongoing Sunday school group.
_____ met at a time other than Sunday morning.
_____ had only one facilitator for this study.

BUSINESS REPLY MAIL

FIRST-CLASS MAIL   PERMIT NO. 22120   MINNEAPOLIS, MN

POSTAGE WILL BE PAID BY ADDRESSEE

Augsburg Fortress

ATTN INTERSECTIONS TEAM
PO BOX 1209
MINNEAPOLIS MN 55440-8807

Edwards Brothers Inc.
Ann Arbor MI. USA
March 10, 2011